The Radiant World

Dan Featherston

BlazeVOX [books]
Kenmore, NY

The Radiant World by Dan Featherston

Copyright © 2009

Published by BlazeVOX [books]

Printed in the United States of America

Book design by Geoffrey Gatza

First Edition

ISBN 13: 9781935402176
Library of Congress Control Number: 2009920366

BlazeVOX [books]
14 Tremaine Ave
Kenmore, NY 14217

Editor@blazevox.org

publisher of weird little books

BlazeVOX [books]

blazevox.org

for Rachel

We appear to have lost the radiant world where one thought cuts through another with clean edge, a world of moving energies, *mezzo oscuro rade* . . .

—Ezra Pound, "Cavalcanti"

Contents

The Radiant World

The Art

Bricklayer's bucket brick trowel rope scaffold pulley
            can't make out the silver square
flashing against his chest
(dog tag? saint x?)
watching him guess the distance—
brick he holds
                              something for the hole
before any of us, any art,
the guesswork.

Narcissus

                        changed to a flower,
everywhere his thoughts
proliferate in seed—
a climate he confuses with himself.

All answers taste vaguely of inquiry.
Image: nostalgia for one's self.

In Narcissus: jonquil, daffodil,
the spectral sadness of Echo
intent upon another's life.

Anagram Sonnets

   1.

Earth's net of reason and
theft. Stone, sea
froth. Not
father
throne.
Fate
the
one raft, net of near. Toad, fern. As shred.
Fasten
red
hat. Fate another fast
end, shatter
of
near.

2.

The nod,
near
that snare
of end. Sea fern
froth. Far Eden,
hot desert. Eden hasn't
that
dense eon's end. Done, then,
as shot raft. Eden
front
a fade. Hades
a shade net.
He sent on
a non.

3.

Draft
sheet. No, a
fetter, a soft forest nest.
Her farthest
end
no farthest
end. Her fond heart
shred
to rend
earth.
Eden a den drone. A raft, then a dent shone.
A heron, a herd sent
on.
A hornet.

4.

Sea tenor. Eden
trash:
hate. Eden
fed
her,
not Satan.
So the
sonnet (shattered
tenor)
sent to thread
Dante's
heft
and soft
tree. Hand.

Vials

Ambergris a brassy pepper soil, gondola's
heaped spice nosing through flannel, cotton
channels, eddies of wooled heat. Is it a slim
sand vitrified? Liquidy pith telescoped in glass?
Essence of x: hint of altitude in a map's flat?

A doorbell dot of vanilla. Behind each ear a pulse
heating the pearl, cream, beige over ambergris'
amber tone, gris dabbled from finger to belly,
each odor's opening like syllable cleated air.

Where does it go, the small stain of her voice?
Her hand's erasure, trill of birds unbuttoning air.
Peeped from vials, columns of rain fall upward,
opening the sill's still keyboard: fugue pipes
glass flutes, her fingers loosing amber into air.

Tube Rose

A sleep walker I have often seen.
She smelt of tube-rose, and sang . . .

—Erasmus Darwin

Perfume Notes

Tuberose's *bit of blue odor*
folded in cobalt crepe.

Sweet clusters at the tip.
Bitter's troughed tongue
slopes throatward.
Bitter V
        convulse, convolute.

As hefted: sweet—light; bitter—heavy.
A prelingual odor
faster than the speed of language.

To fade is fatuous.

•

Lower registers: musk, earth.
Upper registers: jasmine, lavender, lily.
Mishearing gives odor its sweetness.

A forceful fading. A force fading. Protean odor's evanescent
shapes: fire, water, lion . . . Task of holding: the task is
holding to resistance giving forth the right name. A truth
extracted. Attar. Essence: wispy avatars of animal, mineral,
plant.

Lexical Tuberose

A plant with a tuberous root, short, grasslike leaves, and a liliaceous flower; the Polianthes tuberosa.

There is an illustration of the flower beside the entry—sprig of tuberose showing various stages of bud & bloom. Monstrous dictionary flower. Monstrous secrets yielded all at once.

If knobby, then a force revolving.
If smooth, a force resolving.

Blue pith. Already I am seaward or nightward,
far from the flower itself.

Spoken rose elides:
tuberose
tuber rose

Language flower: a trunk branching forth, or a man blowing a tuba. In the alphabetic landscape, a man blows a tuberose trumpet rooted in tube, twisting through lexical derivations—tuba, tuberose, tubercular. A turbid melody cognate with breath's disease.

Form: a terminal force.

Truth Extract

Odor: inference: truth's spectral
essence in lachrymals & vials:
how many flowers to the half-ounce?
what ratio of sorrow to tears?

Each word gathers into its own vanishing,
withering on the stalks of actual objects.
Stalking actual objects,
compression called thinking dissipates,
lost in its own extracts, expressions.

Incommensurate desires:
to describe / to yield to any object as symbol of itself.

Radios

Ponge's radio was a dung heap spread in the sun,
& Lowell's—a bleating box tuned to the dead.

The neighbor's radio is a voice filling empty morning air.
It says *I am not there.*
It says *I am the window you listen through,*
stumbling into noon, rinsing moonlight out of the drapes,
& crank it up to disguise death's amplitude.

That man in the car next to you,
his life is a radio heart
throbbing in death traffic.
But the words are unintelligible,
all bass & trouble & the red light of heaven,
revving to drown out silence—
life's little radius
inside the music of the spheres.

Ornithology

: One might study ornithology & the bird elude him.

: The bird & the study of birds are ordinary things.

: The ordinary's most beautiful—how earth endures itself
in building's brittled sunlight, gecko scuttle under aloe,
these shadows puddled in mortar & bark,
& the wind milled blue through palms.
If only I could lie with you here, now,
& evening come down all around us,
birds pulsing in the open palm of twilight.
Let me trace you everywhere, for isn't love to feel everything
look back as through the eyes of the beloved?

: Earth asks nothing of me & I ask nothing of it.
My reflection breaks with the mirror.
There is no judgment in the earth. Ornithology?
Mere dream a bird's small orbit would brush away.

: But perhaps is just this emptiness, this utter loosing,
where we look, as into a mirror,
& there is no one looking back.

The Piano

after Jane Campion's

Flicker Fusion

the piano inside the boat inside
the ocean inside the cell inside
the piano inside the theater inside
the darkness felt like hammers
felt like oars felt like fusion
inside the piano's flicker fusion
in song light toward shore.

Music

Pythagoras heard music in the spheres
& fashioned a phorminx
from the seven-stringed universe.
Kepler scored it:

    Mercury   soprano
    Venus   contralto
    Jupiter, Saturn   bass
    Earth   mi, fa, mi

misery, famine, misery . . .

    •

The ocean is a piano whose silence is dead weight.
No need for metaphor when the land.
No need for metaphor when the man
speaks for you. Let the piano speak for you.
It is an ocean tugging against the shore
to be a long way off from silence.
To be a long way off from violence.

Film

There is nothing not even
music outside the frame
the camera rocking
boatlike back & forth.

            •

Inside the theater the matinee eclipsed the sun.
Outside the theater the matinee was a marquee's
clock of black letters eclipsed by the sun.

            •

At noon she steps into an eye of coiled rope.
One end is tied to a piano leg.
Through a hole in the black hose
he touches her music.
Through a hole in the music
he touches her skin pretending
silence & the simple clarity of noon.

            •

Piano: the body twists upon itself.
Forte: the rope twists upon itself.

Green

There was a time when everything was green.
Now crimes embrace the trees.
Naturally, money is green.
The principle generates
interest we keep
banking on wilderness.

Puritan Trees

Fill the bucket with soap water.
Scrub lust from the trunks.
These are the instruments of divine transmission—
ears listening between heaven & earth,
unsoiled by human dictation.
This is how we harmonize colonialism & Christian telos.
The end will be a bucket of soap water
in a forest of transparent trees.
We are trying to scrub the earth out of our bodies.

Blue

Through the film's blue filter the piano is a casket.
Through the film's blue filter the piano is a corpse.
Light's muted tones.
A billowing dress.
An opaque note.
Where the sheet's scored daylight falls up through the frames.
Faces sway like watery stems bobbing brightly over the bow.
Is it light or water bending the oars?
Which way is to drown?
The piano lessens, erased under fathoms.
Men & their languages.
It could have been violin, flute, some small buoyancy held in her hand.
A bird.
A bouquet.
Something slender slipped into a case, laced up in a boot.
It could have been the portable instrument of her voice.
She sits down before the piano.
A strip of ivory keys under the door.
The music is an inviting surface.
The music invites surface.
Someone places a rose there.
Someone sets down a tumbler of bourbon.
Parlored evenings parcel out in objects & falling scales.
Each depression turns open a room behind the key.
In its harp-shaped frame she sees acoustic architecture.
A wooden cloud.
A polished cove.
A sleeping animal whose musculature turns inward.
Touched, it twitches.
Some other music.
The piano is difficult to move.
Some aquatic animal.
How will they ever get the music of the ocean into those hills?
Planks & roller wheels lubricate the grade like moonlight.
The island is a house whose windows fill with water.
The piano is boarded up like a house.

His hammering asks *What is this daylight splintering in like ivory?*
It must belong to water—how she plays the table's crayon keys.
Everything vibrates.
Wood—instrument of music.
Remembering the percussive quality of air, how it winced with sound.
Flexing & folding.
Loosed from blue, keys clatter to the surface.
Remembering the resonance of time.
Remembering a residence in time.
Glissando: everything drifts upward into silence.
Through the film's blue filter the piano is an instrument of air.
Through the film's blue filter the piano is an instrument of wood.
Begin at middle sea.
Pian, forte. Pian e forte.

The Lineaments of Gratified Desire

What is it men in women do require?
The lineaments of Gratified Desire.
What is it women do in men require?
The lineaments of Gratified Desire.

—William Blake

THE ARCHITECT dreams of floating temples & gardens,
domes giving suck to sky. Her protean shifts
the blueprint tacked to lumber:
the hip's torque & elbow's crooked sky;
water's splash for brass bangles dangling down;
breasts for shook puddles;
scarves for dervished birds & the pulse of small hours.

THE ENGINEER covets covering, pretending nakedness.
He quarrels with gravity,
secretly in love with her keystone,
her heavenly nadir in stiletto spire.

THE TOURIST points to maps & rubbernecks the rotunda,
calling for coffered heavens
& hobbies including moonlight & beaches,
riding brooms among real horses.

THE LINGUIST tucks Latin into the G-string.
Pluribus Unum: the color of money & sexual arabesque.
It's legal to be tender, stuffing holes,
but men who live under roofs forget the shape of the sky.

THE COUNTERFEITER folds money into animal totems
signifying the distance between desire & possession.
Green means grow forth
from the intersection of artifice & vine,
all debts public & private.

THE INTERROGATOR believes the dance is interrogation.
Her body is information.

Unscrew the obstructions that silence you.
What remains is intelligence.

THE LIBRARIAN finds them shelved under bushes,
dew confused for the pulpy odor of sex.
In the green library, fear fills the trees
with eyes for birds' blind flutter in the leaves.

She finds him studying fear
& burns them in the incinerator.
From a clump of ash he imagines *woman*,
wanting her Alexandria, her heat turned inside out.

THE PRIEST believes truth is to have no body:

Beauty is the circumference of illusion.
It shall be given up.

When supper had ended, transubstantiation was holes & folds.
The magician's rabbit. The Eucharist & the empty tomb
& so on disappearing through her, believing touch was despair:

The book is the body of evidence.
What I desire is beyond you.

THE WINDOW WASHER believes transparency is clarity,
but every story ends in bucket water
flat with afternoon clouds.

Falcons grip her ledges,
waiting for high swallows in the updraft.
From scaffolds, the mortal upshot:
everything pedestrian & gallows humor.

THE LANDLORD worries her cable will snap.
He sees vacancy & the middle sag.
He sees banisters bruised by pianos & dragged suitcases.

THE CARPENTER thinks not mortal stripdown
but the propped façade:
burgundy corset & leather, the boa's painted feathers.

All my life this blueprint of setting forth.

THE DANCER asks what makes the lap dance?
You cannot get beyond surface, which is suffering.
Only the dead are naked & resemble nothing.

Strip's *stroopen* is plundering swift fleets
for holds of gold, cattle head & sweets.
Not strip, poor pirate, looking for rare earth at sea,
gold in them hills, the westward ho & so on.

Wisdom genuflects under my roof beam.
Animals flock to my thighs.
Swaddling is to be enfolded in creation.
If you look closely,
you can see a small nativity in the Bethlehem of my skin.

Those who cannot give birth offer rare earth—
gold & frankincense & myrrh.
They say there is sweetness in my wood.
Or is there only blood's bitter swaddling
& sad allegories of starlight—
nothing in folds but generations unfolding?
Would it really save you to see something not born of death?

Willow

             want's opening to O's
uplifted green bent to bowstring,
flute, language stood supple
& simply itself:
  a dormancy of shapes.

      •

Setting sprays in a vase,
words to spoken wheel,
willow's wilt
        widened to welt
weal   lashed to the turn of water
     a basket,
     a palm,
antenna   tuned to a radio of mud.

      •

Divining "fountain spray"
from *salix*,
        as if under the surface of language
a tree gestures toward itself.

      •

Suppose a willow. Suppose
bent toward reflection:
wind   the reminder of artifice
rooted in atmosphere that adheres
by estrangement,
          tugged toward itself:
ludic C arched toward
O hooded falcon,
   O compass,
      O mirror to complete the project of a face.

•

But the weave of language floats a baby of dubious origin
downstream through channels choked with bulrush,
a wilderness for swaddle.

•

Adopting the other-than-itself: metaphor's intent
of hair, limbs, weeping steeped in gilt spindles
holding a bird with human face: the edenic pond,
the tire swing & willowy women in hoops.
& yet the air's charged yellow there,
diffusing the door
                         her heart opens
intent upon a mirror doused in images,
divining her own face.

Some Lives of Water

All night
rain falling over the house

•

Kettle's
tumbled thrum
drum

•

Stalks stood
in root
scribbled glass

•

One drop:
the whole room dangles there

•

Face floating
raised between
basin & palms

Face falling
broken

•

Some sealed
sweet

Some suckling
spout

Some broken
by light

•

Coiled green
under a bush

•

Ice trayed
staved

•

Turbid
amber
tinted
tumbler

•

All afternoon
rain falling inside the piano

•

Pauses
puddled
light

•

Detective novel's
steam grate

Textbook's
scattered billiard balls

•

Shook belly's hollow
heart of floating soap

•

Nippled hydrant

Eyes sore with looking

•

Solid liquid gas

Fist palm fingers

•

Evening
even the sky
liquid

•

All night
house on fire under an ocean

Thorne Miniature Rooms Exhibit

There will always be more things in a closed, than in an open, box.

—Gaston Bachelard

Outside the Exhibit

rooms—ruse of "open land"

I am distressed if I cannot enter,
distress—a small room
(you get claustrophobic in there).

Find another way.

Let large be
these small invocations.

South Carolina Ballroom, 1775–1839

A room is its objects:
hutch, harp, sideboard, mullion, candelabra.

A room is a door handling
turns through,
        turns the room through you
crossing periodic thresholds:
a doorknob
a dialectic.

A room is a time.

        •

Looking in disturbs what wants no outside—
smooth weather of walls,
acrylic cloud on clapboard . . .

you cannot conceive of infinite space
though these walls imply outside—
destresse
cornered in four-square compression.

        •

A room with a door is unfinished.
A room without a door is unfinished.

Each door removes a room.

Moving room to room
you people it peeking in.

        •

Compressed to iconic vanishing point,
the body is a keyhole
held in Adamah's eye.
Jehovah strolls in the garden,
small pantomime of mind
a stride civil & wild.
His eyes are blind spots
voice would recover,
where "art thou"
sees "thou art" naked,
reversed in thine other's eye.

          •

I want someone in there.
I want is someone in there
making room on the tiny piano,
some vast nonchalance
like roses flung on the divan:
the casual causal,
some small disturbance
pullulating in parlor air.

California House, 1940s

The ocean's tugged syllogism yoked
like a wall between two rooms:
It is evening in the West,
it must be dawn in the East.

Rooms moving clockwise through history's
diminutions—
                        this vast oblivion
we are tired of imitating,
& mimic mimicry:
                        action paintings
for portraits of French ambassadors.

But the walls are always fashionable,
harboring vistas between avocado drapes,
millennial straits:
We can imitate everything but our own looking.

Where the miniaturist lifts out his hand
fiction rushes in.

Poem for January—Month of Doors

New year declares the door, rifle shots like rapped wood
opening a change of face.

•

Pedestrians mill the suck, turns styled
in rubber knocks, glass pods.
No one goes through.
No one turns open like a key, rooting through multiple cells.

•

"The door squeaks" says something about the hinge,
about the turned handle spinning gold loose
under tumbled numbers, an interest compounded
daily round decimals of winced air.
In *crease*, between. An approximate measure
round about & more or less sound.

•

You read the overseas message, turn the knob to haul in the hawser,
hear causal in the messenger's chain
commanding a syntax like braids of seaweed & bad news.

•

Then everything seems part of cog & cause—
swath's old threshing, cut in the buckled floor,
thrown arcs of coming round, bolting out.
Everything handled as instance.

•

Everything handled is instant
turning in thought—
a knob, a new year's asterisk,
soft split in which you place time,
star in the calendar's
constellatus of days.

•

A knock resonates in wood,
hangs a question like a door
opening the *who's there*,
every face a punch line
effaced in pun.

•

Every mask an inversion.
January: Keeper of Doors.
An auspicious time
"when no sweeping is done."

Our Lady of the Phone Booth

Our Lady of the Phone Booth signals through glass. She is a profile of the voice cradled against her ear. Pedestrians decipher her gestures. Buried in the phone booth's transparency, she is visible in every direction but the trajectory of her listening.

•

An odor of rain scatters in the clatter of change falling through the phone.

> *I'm sorry, a coin is not a number,*
> *a number is not a voice.*
> *Please try again.*

•

In her hand the coin is a tambourine locked in ice, a coral-rimmed island, a monocle. Washington's wig floats cloudlike under her thumb. His profile is a pronoun eclipsed in anonymity & speculative dimension. She flips it over. Like any face, it's two-sided, stuffed with antipodal feathers, branches & raised letters.

> *I'm sorry, the number you have reached*
> *exceeds one.*
> *Please try again.*

•

In her hand the coin is hopelessly *pluribus unum,* a thimble of water, a telluric charm tossed into effervescent electrical baths streaming from switchboards. She re-dials; his profile dissolves, particulated through telegraph wire sagging over sage, canyons, probable cattle.

•

The booth's odor of rain may be thoughtful evanescence, high-pressure zones of speculation like who decides the shape of a coin? Who decides what ratios of ore? She opens the *Book of Phones* to "Coins: A Brief History" between "Coffins" & "Coprophilia":

> The first coins were pressed into various homologous shapes: shells, hooves, feathers and teeth. The coins of Atlantis were shaped like sea horses. In Canaan, homunculi. Over time these shapes were worn smooth. The circular coin was adopted, signifying the Eucharist, the moon, or the shapes of certain vowels. Today, coins are comprised of ores to remind people of the earth's alchemy between labor and commodity. They are backed by ghostly gold standards whose genealogy of debt traces back to the dead. Their "flash in the pan" is a pun on "all's excrement."

•

Her coin telescopes to a bird's-eye view of a well. She puts an ear to the cobble. A voice splashes below:

> *What is it you wish?*

•

She may be talking to herself. If someone is listening, her voice is like rain falling all around a man dreaming of icicles & mice:

> *What is it you wish?*
> *To be dissolved in the currency of your voice.*

•

She may be listening to someone. If someone is talking, the voice pulverizes to electrical dust:

> *I miss you, hurry home.*
> *Ibis hue, blurry loam.*

•

Her odor of rain is despair. She sees a confessional in every booth, lattice in the mullion, push-button gematrias. Her voice tripwires through electrical thicket, floats spectral over oceans & continents. When the lines cross, she smells blood, vinegar & lumber.

•

Her odor of rain may be static in the line or the distance between speaker & receiver:

> *A telephone booth is an altar. Your voice is grain on a threshing floor. You are dime thin, slipping into phone booths like Delphic pillars, lingam shrines. That lattice is the pattern of your voice woven through your own listening. You are calling yourself by another's name.*

> *All the same, she says, a phone booth is a cathedral where sanctuary is to be a voice without a face. Who can pin one on the anonymity of these ringing bells? I am only a voice to you, redirecting rain. But hear how it falls in refrain, braided with gravity. This is myself, sluiced through gargoyle pout. Call me Our Lady of the Phone Booth. I'm raining down like mist through all your listening.*

A Book of Dreams

What becomes of the world outside a sleeping body
        : It becomes a lover.
What becomes of the lover inside a sleeping body
        : It becomes a world.

     •

If a woman dreams of a coat turned inside out
        : Then there is weather under her skin.
If she dreams there is weather under her skin
        : Then the world is turned to a net.
If she dreams of a net
        : Then the world is turned to water.
If she dreams of water
        : Then the world is turned to stone.
If she dreams of stone
        : Then the world is turned to air.
If she dreams of air
        : Then the world is turned to a dream.
& if she dreams of a dream
        : Then she is awake.
& if she is awake
        : Then there is weather under her skin
like the dream of a coat turned inside out.

     •

What an owl dreams:
That trees are holes.
That talons are doorknobs.
That the heart of a mouse is a door.
That hunger is unending thresholds.
That a dream is a hole in the middle of a tree.

     •

She went to sleep in the train station
under a statue of Athena:
        a lamp in one hand
        an owl in the other.

Lamp:
She is all departure & arrival.
She sees herself approaching.
The platform empties into her.
She is shelved with luggage, birdcages, boots.

Owl:
She is all aisle—a conductor.
There are tombstones shelved overhead.
Ticket please the part that sticks to her like grief.

Lamp & Owl:
Is an owl a sort of light
        : You mean a transfer.
I don't need a transfer
        : Then you have your own light.
But I am aboard myself
        : Then you confuse yourself with death, as if light were animation.

When the landscape thickens in the glass,
you will empty onto the platform
& scatter in all directions.

Athena:
Are these kinds of light, & wisdom—a fulcrum
        : The lamp is stone & the owl hunts in darkness.

She hunts owls by lamplight.
She calls vision a kind of light—
an owl's or a lamp's panoptics.

Is her body a conductor
          : There are faces leaning in the aisle.
Are rituals kinds of light
          : She is in a wedding dress. She is in a casket.
& the lamp, the owl—is there no other conduct
          : There are flowers growing along the aisle & rails.

When she wakes, her fingers are braided together.
Someone has placed a tiny paper rose at her feet.

          •

If you fall asleep in sawdust
          : You will see your face in a tree trunk.
If you fall asleep on a card table
          : You will live 52 years.
If you fall asleep in hay
          : You will dream of horses.
If you fall asleep on crushed glass
          : You will dream of heartbreak.

          •

   A Book of Laws

Every crime is attached to a hand.
Take soap & scour it.
Cut it loose from the limb.

For thievery, cut off the left hand.
For a repeated offense, cut off the right.
For a third offense, call the body a hand.
Cut it loose from the world.

          •

The prisoners without hands retrace their deeds, moving counter-clockwise under the gun turrets. At all times there is judgment. All time is judgment. Their eyes wince, watching bird shadows pass like hands through barbwire. At the ends of their sleeves there is no evidence. There is nothing to touch. Nothing touches them but the hand of judgment.

•

For a lark the warden hires a palmist who, after several days of confusion & boredom, plays along by reading phantom palms & pulling slivers out of thin air. The thieves are hysterical with laughter. The warden is furious & cuts off their arms at the elbows. When the palmist is caught reading minds, his eyes are torn out.

•

The lovers slept under a common roof,
but with a wall between them.
At night they would meet in the courtyard
& eat sliced pears by moonlight.
She would say: "*Duo* means two, & *plicare* is to fold."
& he: "The sight of an arrow made Zeno grieve;
nonetheless, he was a skilled archer."

When she dreamt of a crying woman,
he dreamt a cacophony of pianos.

•

The somniloquist keeps a parrot named Telephone next to her bed.
Each morning it wakes her with its memory of her sleep.

•

The hunter sews fox fur to the insides of his pajamas
        & dreams he is a winter den.
The grocer sleeps with a coin under his pillow
        & dreams of starched aprons.
The farmer sleeps with an opened almanac under his bed
        & dreams of meteor showers.
The young man, asleep in silk,
        dreams his lover's thighs are milk.
The man who had his wife's corpse stuffed with feathers
sleeps beside her every night,
        dreaming of the aviary where they met.
In a bed made of driftwood, he clings to his lover,
        dreaming of bright coral.

      •

An aquatic scene is painted on the ceiling above the crib.
In the morning there is sand
in the corners of the baby's eyes,
lids blue & swollen like opalescent shells.

      •

Why is a book of dreams
        : To lie between worlds.

A Psychology of Space

The house furnishes us dispersed images and a body of images at the same time.

Place proposed in blueprint blue:
highest register of darkness,
lowest register of light.

Walls of all worth speaking.
Walls of all left to speak
the fact of silence
proposing place.

Words . . . little houses, each with its cellars and gardens.
Common-sense lives on the ground floor,
always ready to engage in "foreign commerce,"
on the same level as the others,
as the passers-by, who are never dreamers.
To go upstairs in the word house is to withdraw,
step by step; while to go down to the cellar is to dream,
it is losing oneself in the distant corridors of an obscure etymology.

House is *to hide* these pleated privacies
in public fabric's fold.

An architecture's listening,
writing into walls
between rooms that fall.

In ancient feeling the privative trait of privacy
meant literally a state of being deprived of something.
A man who lived only a private life, who like the slave
was not permitted to enter the public realm,
or like the barbarian had chosen
not to establish such a realm, was not fully human.

Razed behind the wrecking ball pun,
razed as a wall's two faces.

Where the roof's razed,
blue falls through—
revelation of public sky
raised over every privacy.

It is not a building, but . . . dissolved
and here a bit of corridor which . . .
does not connect the two rooms,
but is conserved in me in fragmentary form.
. . . the whole thing . . . scattered about inside me.

Passing under lintels, Pythagoras would not speak,
held to the threshold of silence between rooms.

The paradoxical strength of passageways—
tense in the wall's braced force,
gravity falling upward in the keystone.

If the child is unhappy
the house bears traces of his distress.

His disavowal of the house—
childish anger rooted in fear.
Anger for having been born
into the house of his own death.
Not devotion. Not genuflection
but stumped. Not stumped
but stooped in misery,
stupefied in mystery,
bent over the knee of father-house.
A pouting gargoyle, jealous of eternity.

The memorial gathers round a vital absence,
gathers a vital absence
as boundary to destruction.

Against memorial, against this absence
he made of his private disdain
a surrogate construction, a private erection
raised in the public place of memorial.

Beware those who do not feel life & death
trembling at the core of all common things.

At the core of memorial, this vital
citizenry of the dead—
specter of collective memory
raised in public monument.

That's the rain. I could be the rain.
That chair—that wall.
I could be that wall.
It's a terrible thing for a girl to be a wall.
& terrible not to be a wall.

So a wind eye in window
& face in each facade.

The house helps us to say:
I will be an inhabitant of the world,
in spite of the world.

Yellow House

A yellow house not yellow
but divisible by weather:
ochre in rainlight,
tawny in moonlight

A yellow house not yellow
but divisible by rooms
in which she moves among herself

•

A dream in an unfurnished room:
If a doorframe, then a chair

A passage
A forfeiture

•

A dream in a furnished room:
If a chair, then a doorframe

A passage
A forfeiture

•

Waking furnishes no answers
but an arrangement of questions
leading back through sleep:
whose hand?
whose scuff in the floorboard?
what radio's blush behind the wall
every thing answering its own distance

•

Portrait

wall's
portent of image

•

There is a pause between certainties,
waking in sheet's scribble—
script of a climate palpable under glass

•

The house a portrait whose empty
rooms tug like small birds
tied to vanishing points

Tied to her fingers
habitable fictions

•

Wine's tinged light in glass ballast,
as if voice were the transparency of face

Room's liquid wobble
the tenuous pulse of speech

•

The whole house humming—
fingerprints rubbed into cupboards,
whorled round sink spigots,
smeared in the wine stem

Towels hung with handling
shadow over folded shadow

•

Anemones open into the mirror's
soft interior,
   entering at angles
     its capsular light

& yet would want, precisely,
the fixed arrangements—
   these twiggish sprays over the bureau,
her fingers unbraiding spaces
between the stems

•

These surfaces—departures
in face, photograph, voice,
as if we come forward facing
always away from ourselves

The porch, lintel & mirror,
the glass photograph miniatures
you'd placed along the sill,
snaring light,
     as if rooms
& the possibility of a door

Wedding Invitation

Procession in profile—
musician holding hollowed
horn must be heavy all that
music blown back from
the small end over his head

No one turned to look behind
that song gets all the way
back into the flag's
red ripple shapely with wind

Painted elephant tusks
rug draped hump
one walks beside another
holding a pole
everyone holding something

Groom up under canopy
holding his thoughts

Is marriage a kind of profile?
Of whom?
Of two?

Under a canopy he thinks
she means all the world
enclosed within its round shadow
Or is thought a profile of the world
half turned toward the thinker,
eclipsing what it would reveal?

What would a marriage of profiles reveal?

One rides the elephant neck
holds something in his hand

     flower?

          some small detail
under a largeness—
procession of details

groom
meditating on an elephant

bride
riding behind him

Meditating on the distance they've traveled
tangents between them their thoughts
traveling tandem

There is marriage in slope & lurch,
wheels turning below them
nothing but these details:
two white bulls yoked mid-step

She between green drapes pulled back
for us to look in?
her to look out?

Marriage opens a veil

Flanked by bulls either side
bright bridled horse
footmen with spears
are these tangents?

Profiled by travel, half-turned
toward what village gate?

We do not enter with hosts of images
but occasional marriages
moving elephantine slurred weight

No ground below there is not even
a path but mere latitude
balanced between animal shoulders
& rickshaw wheels

Where are their belongings?
Who pays the hornblower?

In profile, half secret

All marriages half spectacle
turned toward you who, stopping,
notice everything still proceeds—
green turbans, yellow rope, red sash, blue eyelets . . .
questions
intersecting an answer

Acknowledgments

Thanks to the editors of the following publications, where versions of some of these poems first appeared: *Angle, Antenym, Central Park, Cultural Society, Detroit Metro Times, First Intensity, House Organ, Nedge, New American Writing, Ploughshares, Situation, Sonora Review, Sulfur, Talisman, Tinfish* & the chapbook *Rooms.*

"A Psychology of Space" includes passages from Hannah Arendt's *The Human Condition* & Gaston Bachelard's *The Poetics of Space.*

Dan Featherston's books of poetry include *The Clock Maker's Memoir* (Cuneiform Press, 2007), *United States* (Factory School, 2005) & *Into the Earth* (Quarry Press, 2005). He teaches at Temple University & lives in Philadelphia with Rachel McCrystal & their companions Fredo & Itze.

Made in the USA
Monee, IL
07 July 2026